THIRD MAN BOOKS

TWIN LEAD LINES

POEMS BY
LOU TURNER

for good listeners

You remember songs of heaven
Which you sang with childish voice
Do you love the hymns they taught you
Or are songs of earth your choice?

–Ada R. Habershon, "Will the Circle Be Unbroken"

O for God's sake
they are connected
underneath

–Muriel Rukeyser, "Islands"

Scan the QR code to listen to soundscapes
that accompany certain poems.

Published by
Third Man Books, LLC
623 7th Ave S
Nashville, Tennessee 37203

Art direction: Jordan Williams, Amin Qutteineh
Cover/book design: Amin Qutteineh

ISBN: 979-89-89908-98-1

THIRD MAN BOOKS

thirdmanbooks.com

Table of Contents

will the circle be

The O and the I

1.

I make its shape   in the mouth

Ohh.   (a realization.)
Oh!   (a revelation!)

O, my stars

O, my love

O, my god

O, my soul and body!

O as an orbit
O as a closing
O as an opening

i'll be etheric clew

As a child I joined a chorus calling O's up from a pew
　　　toward the big father O
　　　　　arms cradled above in surrender

O, my God

　　　　　　　　　As I grew I spilled over and down the back alleys
　　　　　　　of understanding, each more liminal, pointing
　　　　　to all I would not be able to learn　　　I did learn
　　　to behold it, my embrace an O around the mystery

O, my stars

I met a writer there whose O was broken on his typewriter
　　　so he used a Ø, certain they held the same value
　　　　　and that was when I knew we really had something to work with,
　　　　　　　my hands shaping an O around his ear as I whispered

O, my love

　　　　　　　　　Can I write a book with more O's than I's
　　　　　　　more outputs than inputs
　　　　　oh, but there I go again
　　　　still negotiating my language within
　　　the binary　　　　all 1's and Ø's
　　no, I write for an encounter of the O and the I
or as my mother says when most surprised

O, my soul and body!

2.

Between semesters,   I see Papaw for Christmas.
How's Nashville treatin' you?   I begin talking about music, so much
of it, how I can open the window and breathe it in,   all shapes, colors
and sizes of it   how this means I've found a home.

Be careful, he says. *You know my cousin Little Jimmy Dickens
moved to Nashville and fell into partying on Broadway.
Drinkin' and all that.*

Little Jimmy Dickens?   I repeat,
the name funny,   too alive in my mouth
        like pop rocks.

Yep, we grew up together running around the holler.
He chased me with a knife one time!
He could be real mean,   he winked.
But oh boy,   *he became a big time country star.*

I'd never heard the word *hollow* spoken by a West Virginian before:

holler.

How does a place become an utterance?

How does a home give way to a yell, a cry — an *O?*

Little Jimmy from the holler chasin' Papaw with a knife. Little Jimmy in the kitchen hollerin' on 'bout an old cold tater. Little Jimmy hollerin' on the radio in Beckley, West Virginia. Little Jimmy headed for Nashville with his guitar. Little Jimmy never world famous but always a big star. Little Jimmy's songs pitched to Hank Williams who could really make them sing. Little Jimmy standing on the stage long after Hank, all four foot eleven inches,   hollerin'

I'm Little But I'm Loud!   *I'm poor but I'm proud!*

Little Jimmy: the oldest member of the Grand O le Opry
'til he was hollowed out by death.

He sang of humble beginnings in hits like "Take an Old Cold 'Tater and Wait"
and "Country Boy," in which I can see a root of my Papaw's disapproval:

"I raise Cain on Saturday and go to church on Sunday"

Was the cain-raisin' irredeemable in the eyes of Papaw? What about the rest of the family?
Was it where Little Jimmy hollered off to that rendered him lost, or what he hollered about?

Amid the cain-raisin' he cut gospel songs like "Are You Insured Beyond the Grave" and "The Bible on the Table and the Flag Upon the Wall" — songs that I cut apart and paste back together again. Songs I stitch new meanings into. Songs I hollow out for a holler, for something hallowed.

Little Jimmy sang the O in the country song
and the O in the hymn.

I crow the O in the folk song
crown the O in the sonnet.

re-utter ghost-hythe, wingsing

somehow rendered us songbirds

hOller

hOme

hOllow

hOld

hOpe

hOly

rows where some red birdsongs end

Based on word-of-mouth ancestry, Little Jimmy and I were third cousins.
If we both left home to make music in Nashville, does that make us
related by more than blood?   Related *beyond the grave?*

I attempt an answer by trying to write songs as funny as his
without the knee slapper elbow jabber good ole boyhood bent.

I write these poems and Little Jimmy appears —
        taunting me to say something
                            little and loud   right back.

Are You ~~Insured~~ Beyond ~~the Grave~~

Performed by ~~Little Jimmy Dickens~~
~~If the Lord should call today would you be ready~~
~~Or has Satan~~ got ~~you marked as his slave~~
~~It is nice~~ to be ~~insured while we are living~~
~~But are you insured~~ beyond the ~~grave~~
~~Nearly everyone has~~ insurance
salesmen ~~sell it~~ every day
~~And my Friend I'm~~ an insurance salesman
~~but in a different sort of way~~
I'd like ~~to tell you about soul's salvation~~
something that ~~everybody needs~~
~~and it~~ doesn't cost ~~you one single penny~~
~~you just get down on~~ your knees
~~and you say oh Lord~~
~~I want a policy to save my soul from~~ hell
to lift ~~me~~ up from the ~~depths of sin~~
~~with Thee I want to dwell~~
~~and then He'll mark it paid thru eternity~~
~~and no~~ collect~~or will ever~~ call
~~for when Jesus died on Calvary's cross~~
~~he paid the price for~~ all

ready

to be

beyond

Courtesy of the Country Music Hall of Fame® and Museum

If It Ain't One Thing It's Another

does
your grin
ever
grow grim
cold ones clink-
king either ear-
nest boy   did
legends size
you   up
and   down
their tales as tall
as your dreams
tell me a story
about show business
boys   who
saw   the   light

A Sonnet of Things I've Learned from Little Jimmy Dickens

1. The Ancestry.com free trial will charge $39.99 when you forget to cancel it.
2. Freemasonry seems nefarious, but it's actually just out-of-touch and boring.
3. The adjective highfalutin, meaning uppity, may also be spelled high falootin.'

4. Etymologists suggest the root word is *flute*, confirming my suspicions.
   (I play the flute, so Jimmy would've found me high falootin,'
   though I avoid the word *flautist* for fear of being so.)

5. A mausoleum is a filing cabinet for the dearly departing, usually from some falootance.
6. A crypt can also be called a *niche*. His is only a two minute drive from mine.

   Taped to his memorial plaque were fake flowers and a card from his family –
   inside, they shared with him who won the World Series last week.
7. Too bad Atlanta was his team; but Jimmy loved baseball, like me.

   I already knew this one:
   Writing about people, however much you like them, feels dirty.
   Can you pay respects with empty pockets?

Duet with Little Jimmy Dickens in the Key of O

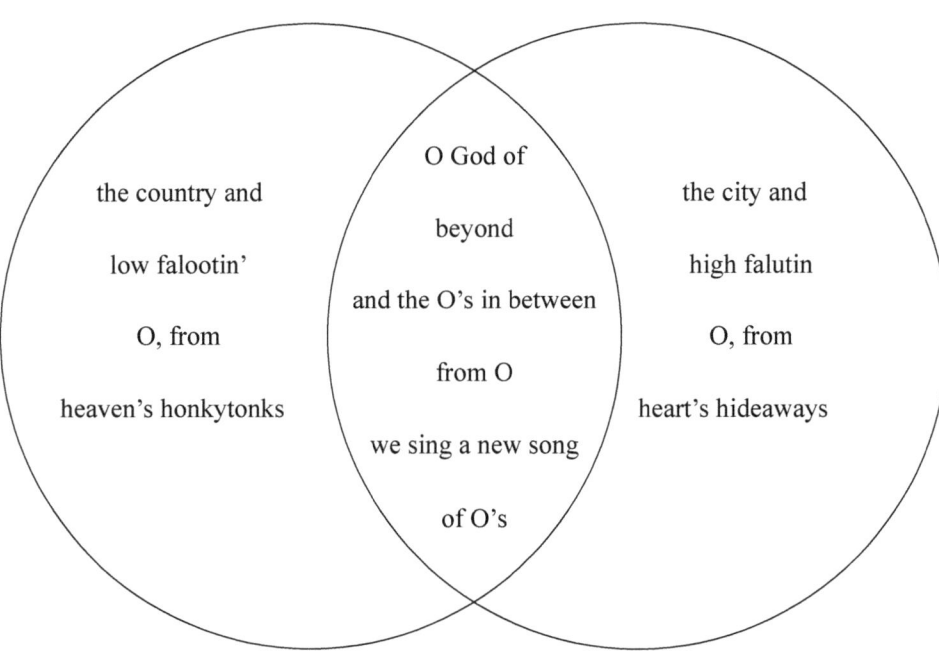

the country and

low falootin'

O, from

heaven's honkytonks

O God of

beyond

and the O's in between

from O

we sing a new song

of O's

the city and

high falutin

O, from

heart's hideaways

i clink in clairaudience

Song Cycle

I'm new to the neighborhood
Who is listening for the cicadas?

In search of a sound mind
God, the denial of denial

Neighbors side-eye the overgrowth
I try to learn all their names

Each month more lilies sprout
Neighbors side-eye the overgrowth

I try to learn all their names
I sing myself in circles

I'm new to the neighborhood
Each month, more lilies sprout

Who is listening for the cicadas?
In search of a sound, mine

God, the denial of denial
I sing myself in circles

i incircle kin, u in a candle

It's not that I expect your heart, but something beating

besides your fist on your chest (we get it, you're little but you're loud).

Something thrumming in the dust of sheet music I thumb through,

something suppressed in the swoop of your autograph, some strain in

the digital grain looping,   some recognition of the stories

I heard from my Papaw. He said you were mean – but once, when I was a child,

shy and inconsolable – he called me mean, too.   Sometimes mean

means hurt. It's not that I'm expecting to hear your hurt, but some kind of singing

where songs fall silent.   In 1986, a single mother was jailed for 99 days on account

of her account being empty. Soon as you and Mona heard, you drove downtown

in your black limousine, paid her bail.   *This wouldn't have happened*

if she was part of the elite,   your manager said to reporters on your behalf.

Did you only like attention on stage? It's not that I'm expecting your voice

    but a way to listen.

Cul De Sac

In the sixth grade when girls
began longing publicly for boys
and privately for each other
I only knew how to want White Jesus
I'm not kidding –
      he was really my boyfriend

I insisted the first band I was in
be called One Way
and even wrote us a song
there's only one way
      and that's His way!

The subject matter suited
my controlling front person
approach perfectly –
and when I booked our first show
on the balcony of my grandparents' house
the only other song in our repertoire
      somehow was "Wild Thing"

But it worked because
it was only three chords
plus, Jesus made my heart sing –
if there were ever a good
and faithful servant
      O, she would've been me

The Bible   **The Flag**   **The Wall**

the Bible
the flag
the answer to it all

the
businessmen
all agree

on the wall

God
what a price   to pay

to
find salvation

Hey Good Lookin'

"Country music is three chords and the truth."
– Harlan Howard

Once, Hank Williams told Jimmy that he needed a hit,
and proceeded to write "Hey Good Lookin" in 20 minutes

The next week he recorded it for himself, teasing
that it was too good after all for Jimmy's short shelf

and while I genuinely do dig its lilting tune, it's a hit
that gets at what I hate most about those hit-on dudes

and 20 minutes is longer than it takes most cats
to think up something cocky to call out and quack

Hey hottie in the kitchen, can I have a little bite?
double-dipped entendres, yum yum, and the like

I went on tour for five days and came home sick of
the same number of cover versions of that shtick

The sound guy called me *hun* but called the other dudes
hey you; then the man after the show who said *so good,*

but you really need to let it loose! several times,
his brow furrowing more with each repeated line,

the other three I'll omit for being commonplace, blasé –
What's that saying again? Three chords and a cliché?

Instructions for Writing a Country Song in Music City

"Come take a listening walk and admire your hand twisting."
— Fred Moten

This town constantly reminds you that country music is "three chords and the truth."

So, to write a country song in Nashville, you must sound out the truth.

First, with a guitar in hand: move downtown; your ears an open mic for the music of the city.

Each time you encounter a loud sound (construction noise, bachelorette party, etc.)

tune a string of the guitar to its pitch; twisting the tuning key until it resonates.

Repeat five more times (once for each string) until you've tuned the guitar.

For lyrics: collect words from passersby, billboards, and other musicians.

Using your voice, string these true things into something you can sing.

Continue, while strumming three chords of your choosing (do not adjust the tuning).

If you do not know any chords, create them: using your fingers

along the fretboard, making any shape that seems to suit the song.

One Side of an Interview with the Ghost of Little Jimmy Dickens

after Hanif Abdurraqib

Q: What was your favorite guitar to play?

For its sound or to contrast your frame?

What made you feel smallest?

Did it upset your mama when you left?

Do you think you would've been a coal miner if you stayed?

Did fame ever give you the feeling that you were being mined?

Will the circle be unbroken?

What was the first song you played after surviving the plane crash?

Will the Circle Be Unbroken?

What's it like to walk away from wreckage unscathed?

Were you aware that you were the first country singer to circle the globe?

What's Country?

What country?

Who gets to circle?

What's at the center?

What was the first song you sang for the soldiers in Vietnam?

What's it like to walk away from wreckage unscathed?

What went unsung?

i save myths, invoice icons

A Ballad on the Backside

When asked about the hits,
Jimmy explained he'd been
branded a novelty singer
for doing the funny tunes,
but he always had a ballad
on the B-side. For every
"May the Bird of Paradise
Fly Up Your Nose"
there was a "My Eyes
Are Jealous," for every canary
its coal mine, every cocky crow
a true blue bellowing croon:

When I look at you my eyes
are jealous of each other
for the beauty they behold

Were the two sides of his singles
jealous of each other? When I
watch the interview I begin to sink,
sensing he felt misunderstood, 'til
I see his sparkling eye, smiling
out the side when he says it:
The deejays always knew me
as the little funny guy – no regret
in his voice, only double-sworded
intelligence made sharper against
itself, made sharper for sheathing.
With the flip of a record, laughter
leading to leaky-sneaky tears,
there was no punchline to be found,
only a holy, lonely sound –

Twin Lead Cable

Two unique strands of copper. Held apart, together. To conduct something else. Little Jimmy and I on either end of a wire – on either end of the twentieth century. Volunteering for local radio, transmitting signals. He was a kid, and his uncle needed a rooster to crow at dawn on WJLS in Beckley. *I can cock-a-doodle-do that,* he said, hitching a ride into town from his holler every morning. I deejayed for Nashville's community radio station, hitching an astral ride on Dorothy Ashby's harp with a show named after Sister Rosetta Tharpe, itching to broadcast the underground into up-above air. Copper may be cheap, but it's highly conducive to electricity. I shorted out when my cost of living no longer left time for record crate scavenging or radio wave gathering. When asked about his time as a radio rooster, Jimmy said, *"Yes, those were good days. We didn't make any money, we weren't there for that, we were just on air, you know."* We both were, you know. Just on air, not putting on airs. We were the roost, howling O's into the night air's indifference.

cock-a-doodle-dooooooooooooooooooooooo

up above my head I hear music in the air, oh, yeah,

Twin Lead Lines

*After the dual lead guitar parts of Little Jimmy Dickens' band The Country Boys,
in which two lead guitars played simultaneously, the second as harmony (usually
beginning on the third note above the melody).*

that good kind / of proud sound / kind and good / some proud kind / of good sound
kinda good that / sound of pride / good and kin / kind of pride / sounds off good

when something means / something for me / I know that / it can mean / something for you
means something when / I'm for something / that knows I / mean it and / you're for something

good days when / not for money / we made music / nothing for money / good fun then
win days good / money for naught / music made us / money for nothing / than good fun

I like to feel / I'm the same / as you know / pretty much any / body else is
to feel like I'm / the same as I / know you are / any one pretty / is a self's body

every time I / go onstage feels / like the first / time on that / stage for me
I time every / feel onstage go / first it's like / that only time / I'm for stage

Will The Magic Circle of Infinity Be Unbroken, Too?

I'm not the only tourist waiting for the doors to open
at the music museum in the old Gap at the Charleston mall.

S is friendly and earnest, a huge Bill Withers fan, but he loves
Jimmy, too – he's even covered his songs, in fact –

did I know Jimmy had grown up across the mountain from Bill,
and did I see Bill's painting of "Grandma's Hands," hanging just there?

His museum pace quickly outsteps mine as I halt
before a four foot eleven mannequin wearing one of Jimmy's suits.

For what feels like infinity I behold each rhinestone, eyes trailing down to
the boots, they're really what get me, how grand and yet small,

I would've outgrown them by the sixth grade, and then I look
up, and at my eye level, also in the glass case, hanging just above the suit,

a musical score, but not Jimmy's, something avant garde – the staves
forming a circle – shining in its laminated plastic it reads, "The Magic Circle

of Infinity" by George Crumb, a fellow West Virginian, from his *Makrokosmos* –
I feel it spin out of the glass and crown me with belonging. I'm among

my own, a communion of those who were also outside or alone, each of us
rooted to this place, country, each of us strange, named for our littleness,

our crumbs, it was all a feast – and suddenly Jimmy begins to play over
the speakers, and S turns to wink, my fellow stranger turned friendly road guide,

walking over now, just as my partner walks in to join me, and S begins to ask:
Were we musicians, what did we play, and wow, we were *both* musicians?!

well, *wow*!

occasional turns to me no longer   meeting my gaze   but looking me up

and down again,

then back over to my partner, because hey, what kind of guitar strings does he like to use?

Have you noticed that when dudes that play guitar get together they can't shut up?

S dares to ask *me* –
                    ("dude that plays guitar" practically my very gender!)

My partner cringing,   reiterating,   *we play together in the same band,*

but it became clear to S that I was not his peer,   so I shuffle away,

buy a postcard, wonder:

Would Jimmy have treated me the same way?

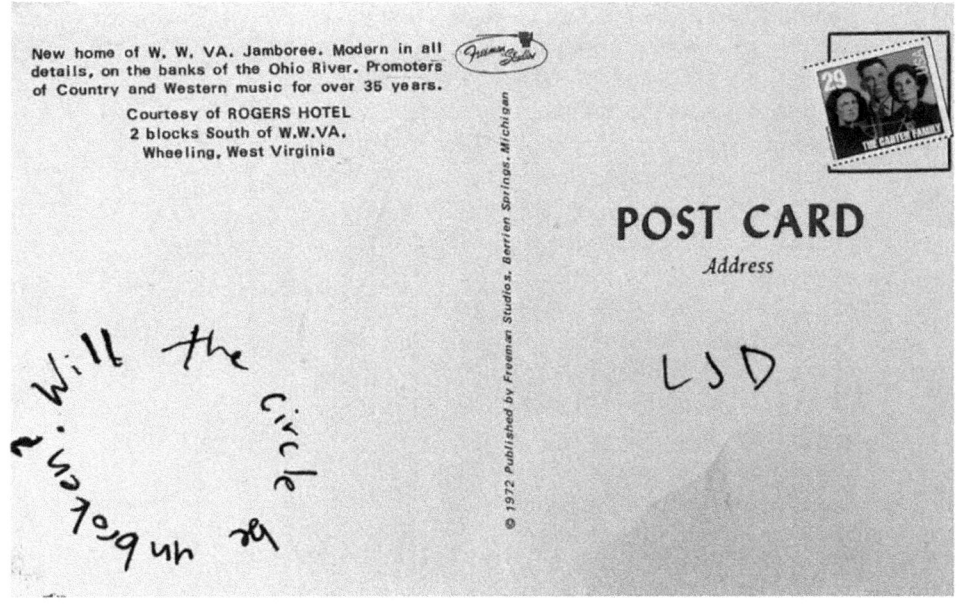

New home of W. W. VA. Jamboree. Modern in all
details, on the banks of the Ohio River. Promoters
of Country and Western music for over 35 years.

Courtesy of ROGERS HOTEL
2 blocks South of W.W.VA.
Wheeling, West Virginia

© 1972 Published by Freeman Studios, Berrien Springs, Michigan

POST CARD

Address

LSD

Will the circle be un broken

Saturday with Mall Jesus

I take him up on that walk through the valley
of the shadow of death, Victoria's angels flitting
overhead and the Hot Topic neon flickering
below – I take his hand and look for the scars,
and when he offers me a slice
of food court pizza – I take and eat,
ask him if it's his body. Ask him how it feels
to be in the movies. I demand to know the real
son, none of this glossy pin-up christ business.
I'm looking to settle down, start
a revolution. At some point he recoils,
citing trouble with overhead;
stammers that he wasn't, like,
God's *actual* son. He becomes insistent
upon distracting me, he'd like to treat us
both to the fish foot spa, and he can
even multiply them like he did back in the day;
and well, I'm almost convinced, but I
just need a minute. I have to use the bathroom.
When I return to his massage chair, he's fled –
only a small, leather-bound signed copy of the New
Testament left in his place, silvery-slivered pages gently
jostling around to the rhythm of the rolling setting.
I sit down, flip the book open, surprised to find
I'm delighted to read his stories over again,
without him there hovering over my shoulder,
or asking for a detailed book report
or commissioning me to sell copies.
No, at last I see the stories as just that,
unadorned and shot through
with chasmic, blossoming holes –
about as big as the ones in his hands,
which really had been so big, hadn't they?
I almost could've slipped my own hand
through and reached to the other side –

His High Note Was My Low Note

after Diane Seuss

I was Jimmy's shiniest rhinestone.
Came to America in Nudie Cohn's pocket,
made my Opry debut stitched onto Jimmy's.
When those lights hit me I wailed.
That aura was all baptism.
Even the lint held a luminescence.
I learned everything about making it big
for how small you are.
He careened on the waves of each laugh,
sang three part harmony with god and the devil.
Got so worked up once he knocked me clean off
and sent me on my way between the floorboards.
I met all manner of show biz folk down there.
The kind you don't read about in the paper,
everybody two or three shades jaded.
Never thought I'd meet a single rarefied soul
who didn't adore Queen Dolly
'til I came across an old tangled hair piece.
Guess the pressure got to her.
She was way wigged out.
When they sawed a circle in the stage
to move the Opry over to the mall, I fell through
the joists and down into another circle of hell.
They say Jimmy passed through here not long ago.
He told a few jokes for the folks before
balladeering his way upstairs. I can't
complain. Takes every last rhinestone
to sell America its own people's music.

Autumn Elegy for Who I Never Knew

burnt ember air the thickening agent
quickening thin space between us

your bald spot my spiritual nest egg

hatched from your crowings-on
trailing your rooster's tail

sweetly speckled sickle

I inherit this hard work, no trickle-
down bootstrap-up boy love

my prodigal patriarch

I crunch marigolden tones underfoot
they still come up sunny sided and singing

a mid-air memorial mural for you

Magnolia Sapling

for Mamaw

My beloved and I spend our breakfast determining
the best place to plant the magnolia tree.

I tell him they're your favorite, or at least
that's what I always heard from Dad.

There must be so many favorites I don't know.
I know you in the space you made for all our favorites:

green beans stewed in bacon fat, rum cake in a bundt pan, not busting
Papaw when you found his not-so-diabetic-friendly candy

stashed in the glove compartment. When I think about you
all the stories are filled   with your filling:

your father passing, your mother needing you
to help raise your sister, to pick cotton to pick

up on everything — you loving   you praying   you
picking grapefruits in the front yard   placing them

next to buttermilk in the fridge   a strange thing   I thought
only sipped in tall tales   you poured in a tall glass

for breakfast.   *It's filling,* you'd say.   We dig
a hole in the yard big enough for your favorite   to fill.

Listening to the Harvest

Harvest sounds *hearty,* sounds sure of itself — sounds like the record, sounds like "Heart of Gold," but even then, Neil sings that it's the *searching* for the heart of gold, and the more I harvest the more I realize I am searching, it is work: it is being harvested by insects, poked by thorny leaves, discerning the green of a bean from the green of a leaf, determining the shine on the skin of a jeweled eggplant — it's finding everything in its exact time, plucking it from this into that — playing god, obeying God, in service of the harvest, on my knees, leaning into the garden, really prostrate before the growth, in adoration of the land — I learn to reap without violence, listen without taking, I yield in more and more colors. Eat with the salt of each season.

What if

we aren't really related
after all this
listening to you
excavating through
records – vinyl, historic, ancestral-ephemeral
tracing fathers of coal miner's daughters
I may never learn how many times
removed
from you

I am

I don't feel

I am

removed
from you
I may never learn how many times
tracing daughters from coal mining fathers
ephemeral-ancestral, historic, vinyl records
through excavating for you
listening to you
after all –
we're really related, aren't we

Theories of Relativity

What if instead of family trees we charted family circles,

    not one another's offspringing branches –

              look – it looks like you!

but timeless orbs

    blobbing into one another's embraces.

Might be going out on a limb here,

    but if you ask me, trees shouldn't have to bear

      the weight of our symbolism anymore, anyway.

And yet. I do come from y'all,

         and it's not that you're so high above me,

but you're rooted down below me, too,

    and that's its own circle

        spinning itself unbroken.

J&J's Market and Cafe

Peggy paints Nashville's buildings before they get torn down. The one of J&J's Market and Cafe has bits of glass she found in the street and stuck in the canvas, as well as a tiny bit of a mirror: *You can find your eye in the reflection there – you'll know it's your eye when you blink!* she says. I find my nose ring first, shining on Broadway where the pedal taverns probably are now. I show her my tattoo of the J&Js sign. She says, *That's an acute angle on an acute thigh!* We eat our fish with melted butter and discover that we both love hymns. Later, when we sing "Will the Circle Be Unbroken" she thinks of her mother, who passed on a *cold and cloudy day* just like it says in the first verse. When I sing that song, I think of Willie Nelson and Venn diagrams. *I'm always thinking of Venn diagrams,* I tell Peggy. She reaches over the table and picks up a beautiful box with three intersecting circles painted on it and she says, *Like this?* I tell her about John Venn, who was a priest before he decided to be a mathematician instead. I ask her if she's heard the verse in some versions of "Will The Circle Be Unbroken" that talks about singing secular songs after being raised to sing hymns. I try to paraphrase it, but I'll include it here now: *You remember songs of heaven / Which you sang with childish voice / Do you love the hymns they taught you / Or are songs of earth your choice?* We drink sangria and sing Peggy's song "Dark Reverie," which she's quick to point out is not a reverie at all. She won't let me leave her house without giving me dessert, and spoons cherry yogurt all over cheesecake like a total genius. I eat happily.

After 96 Years of Business, Brown's Diner Begins Serving Impossible Burgers

But I always had a bit of an authenticity complex,
plus, D the waitress whispers, *that's not real Brown's.*
and when my town has built an empiric tourism industry
around "authenticity" – something they stole to begin with –
it's hard to smell the stakes through mouthfuls of fake blood.
Even Brown's changed ownership recently and began renovation.

I do wish to do better for my body, for every
body, to do right by every chestnut-spotted hide,
to behold it quivering over muscle, not printed
on synthetic leather into a bedazzled cowpokery.
Legend has it Nanci Griffith used to bring her own
shrimp for the spitfire to fry on the grill just for her.
All that singing about finding love at the five and dime, but
she knew sometimes you've got to arrive with an agenda.

Part of me wishes to keep this all a delicious secret, but also
to keep the place in business — watch a gaggle of bachelorettes
tip the band, fall for D. When she brings burgers to their table,
she uses her pointer to caress each colorful plastic flag
and emphatically whispers *toothpick!* almost always
repeats how she's seen one too many accidents.

How many beans can a transplant spill about a hole-in-the-wall
before that wall gets knocked down, paved over,
its regulars unable to get a stool? But hey, not here, not
yet. The new owners seem to have preservation in mind,
shoring up the ceiling so it doesn't cave in, plus a nice
new patio. The other day, on one of the fresh cut benches
a child scooted himself right into a splinter, promptly after
a slew of ants had discovered his ketchup spill, their
wriggling red bodies uncannily close to camouflage,
nearly launching a parade float onto a french fry.

The more time I spend in this town, the more I understand
someone's parade is usually someone else's sticky mess.
Of all my wishes for Brown's, I mostly wish to roll out
the red carpet for each ant we'll later squash unknowingly —
we'll never know what the hell we're doing here
nearly as well as the ants seem to –
their only agenda? Community and labor
married into one marching movement.
Just the thought of all that work and I'm tired, so hungry —
and you know what sounds really good?

The End

It's called The End, and it's beginning to feel like it.
The marquee was gone for awhile, leaving the graffiti'd
concrete square to speak for itself, tucked between
high-rise condos and overdressed pizzas.
We come back because The End hasn't ended, yet,
still stinking out beer and sweat as we duck into
its dark roost, still one blown speaker and still piss
on the toilet seat though you're the first to use it.
The audience is we who play for one another,
we who listen, we who listen to the room as we sing
  Will the Circle, Will the Circle, Will the Circle
Then, the circle widens: the quartet unfurls notes
never strung together before, that will never be
heard again. They quote the past with a question mark:
  Be Unbroken? Be Unbroken? Be Unbroken?
The crushed red velvet curtain ruched behind them
has hung for decades, and the kid running sound
tried three dented microphones before this one — still
slightly bent, leaning into the horn as if receiving a secret
too sweet to keep while here — at the beginning of the end.

Springwater

Lifers, we call us, work our day jobs
then go to the local watering hole to play,
thirsty or overflowing, or sometimes in
between, we are fed from the in-between,
where time is measured in units of three songs.

O, Springwater, oldest bar in Tennessee –
built as a supper club for construction workers
while they crafted a replica of the Parthenon
next door. Next, a refuge for the hard hats
working our jewel-encrusted underbelly
of the music industry – constructing myths
we now continue to maintain – ours not
mimicking the Greeks but just as tragicomic

in a splash-zone-addicted world
paying less than a cent per stream,
we go to the spring –
pay in beer foam and jukebox joist
and O, we pay in attention –
we listen for the flow of lifers,
bubbling up out of nowhere.

We the Roost

We rise, our nest dappled with first light,
    spool into the day wings tendriled mid-air,
moneying as we must but never as we might
    have monied had we less fruit to produce,
had we less eggs to hatch, had we more fear
    of flight. When we go out, we meet in a mass
of multifocal murmuration mid-sky, in time
    for rush hour traffic to tune into our togethering,
transcendent by turns and then scattering, random,
    like ashes, like sun through a crack in the covering.
We peck at our pick of the leftovers, a constellation
    of coin-collecting — enough. Then, we set the table
for our true feast: each feather shed over the day woven
    into a quilt for the night — roosting into so much nothing.

O's Poetica

Like the bird's nest in the VALERO sign,
I've been making home in the O's I can find.
O, when I in awesome wonder consider how
insects frighten me, so beneath me, yet infinite –
armored and attentive. O, to have antenna that dial
directly to your cosmic radio, O — all signal, no static.
O, to be a blade of grass expecting nothing of the morning
but dew. To hit empty and pull into that station
and O, to be filled!
To act like the hunger is real.
O, to know that the hunger is real.
To respect the hunger as real, armored,
and attentive. O, to be so certain of the darkness
that you can close your eyes, fall asleep, and be free.

*

How do you close your eyes, fall asleep, be free
of the neon, though it plays upon your eyelids
like the ominous green sprawling behind the weatherman
pointing: *O, there's a chance, if you chance it,*
could be chancey. O, to be illuminated by the neon
at all! O, world under spotlight. O, world interpreted.
World spinning on the axis of the weatherman's tongue,
world measured on the axis of the marketplace plunge,
measuring worth in the Ø's that it finds,
where the higher the hat the closer to God,
where the measurement of a cowboy hat is called a
crown – another word for a series of sonnets –
but songs don't belong to one royal head, they're sung
in a round – the narrative loops unto the O's that we find.

*

When the narrative loops around the O's we find,
no one sings O the same way, each mouth its own
temporary crash pad for O, bedded down for a night
and then gone before dawn's insistence on light
and light. No one cries O the same way, each O
its own host and transmission, its own portal,
O stars O love O God O soul and body
the O jolting perception awake and awake
another morning to eddy through, another day.
Our brushes with O magnetizing us toward another.
Lose your O and the world is solely a marketplace.
Gain the whole world and lose your O, my soul.
Harder for a rich man to enter the kingdom than
for a camel to move through the O of the needle.

*

For a camel to move through the O of the needle
I reckon there be a reckoning: a transformation
of riches. A wealth of forgiveness,
an abundance of mud baths, a believer's
baptism. A rich man rolling in the soil
might enrich his soul, after all.
O doesn't quite accommodate but it does
shapeshift to revelate. Through the VALERO sign,
through the holes that it finds, blowing them
over and singing, fluting out and through.
O weaving breath through the holes of the
interpreted world, O crowning through the
sonnet and crowing through the country song
bootscootin' our way through eternity again.

*

Bootscootin' our way through eternity again,
we so often lose our sense of by-and-by
and instead we buy-and-sell, take one to-go,
terrified of zero, we leave no room for O.
It takes discipline to craft these odes, to mind our O's
over matter, to make do with our inheritances,
however strange or estranged, to rearrange
and make room for O at center stage,
to acknowledge the mistakes waiting in the wings,
to play in twin lead lines with every soul
along the way. Even a circle must be made up
of intertwined lines, I's forming O's each time
we pray, or say one another's names,
we bear witness to O, a translucent testimonial.

*

To bear witness to O, a translucent testimonial,
making meaning at the bottom of the barrel.
O, making meaning, O, digesting what you eat.
O, a dream digesting the day nourished in sleep.
O, making meaning without explaining what O
means. O, the knowing of meaning that runs deep.
You know O or you don't. You don't think yourself
awake. You wake or you don't. You know or not.
You know O or you don't. You don't eat yourself
alive. You're born or you're not. You sing O by
breathing. You know O or you don't. You don't
truth yourself true. You tell it like it is. You
know O or you don't. You don't sing yourself
loved   you are loved into singing.

*

Love   you are loved   into singing.
Baby   you were born believing.
When O in awesome wonder considered me
I considered awesome wonder back
baby back before time regimented our care
into moments, eggshells, and rime.
I pull into the station each time you say
my name, needle rising up past empty.
This needle pointing toward an O the rich man
might move through if he would only tune in
to that cosmic radio, transmit the by-and-by,
adjust his armor to allow for an antennae. O,
may we each make a home in the O's that we find
like the bird's nest in the VALERO sign.

Without O

all is expected   tempered in gray

tight-lipped   zipped-up

air   tight

calendar squares   garishly grid

the days with   disquieting ease

straightening the   curvature in awe

the serpentine   in sighs

the chasm   what will never be

Without I

no one home nope no one to see here nope not me
love your
god love
your men
love your
self small
and softer
and softer
remember
who oops
no whose
you are no
don't love
you cannot
be trusted!
no one can see me no one can know me nope not me

Without U

almost forgot   impossible

certainly   to say how

that secret   we hold

third thing   love

carries thee   so close

and I   O

closer

Making Do

how do we
do it
we do
however
we must
for the love
of making

make it
make sense
make a wish
make shift
make up
make good
make do

Before the glass breaks, a toast

sometimes my love and I are so broke   we let it all break

   down   open up the cupboard   reach all the way

back   remind one another   *expiration is a lie invented*

by the big business boys   most of the time

      getting paid in units of fear   of time passing

      most of the time   we make enough to make it

most of the time   we make something good

held together by pantry   staples   and what we pull

    out of the yard   we withstand the weather

another winter   we try   to take jobs   that don't

    take from us

when we spend   baby   we spend big

      we make a main course   from sides on the sides

   of sides

    when we drink

      we have something to toast

we spend our days   like we've saved them up

    through the ages   just to live

    in our once-upon-a-time   bodies

Small Ball Heaven

Jimmy, called little on earth, and me, who felt too big in it,
meet up at the family reunion in a nonbinary cartoon heaven,
watch our favorite team of earthlings play baseball on the big
screen, munch sustainably sourced buffalo chicken dip,
pick our sustainably sourced rosewood guitars between bites.
Because we're in heaven, we never sling a stray note –
but if we had, you can imagine how angelic we'd be about it.
We split solos like swirls of relish and mustard on ball park franks.
We love it best when the earth boys play small ball, hot-blooded
home-run hunger cooled into blunt-bunted sacrifice. How bound
by gravity they are! How bound by binary. Earth boys only.
Jimmy doesn't call me *babygirl*. He looks me in the eye.
When he shakes my hand, we realize they're the same size.
Awful for playing guitar, we admit, but tethered by whatever
sized mind it takes to decide to do the hard shit anyway.
In the bottom of the ninth, down ten, we never flip the channel.

My Life is Flying to Your Life

after Muriel Rukeyser

I thought I was going to the church but I am   *behaving more than believing*

    going to the school

I thought I was going to the school but I am   *critiquing more than creating*

    going to the artists

I thought I was going to the artists but I am   *lofting more than loving*

    going to the family

I thought I was going to the family but I am   *solving more than singing*

    going to the honky tonk

I thought I was going to the honky tonk but I am   *believing more than behaving*

    going to the church

Still on the Line

What is it about Glen Campbell's Wichita Lineman
cued up everyday for months on end, I can't imagine
a day without longing for its soft mellow whine, in its
essence, a whistle-while-you-work-song, wishing for

vacation, wishing for your work to align you with
another, and the song actually did that, penned by
Jimmy Webb and covered by everyone from The Meters
to REM to Z and J at our wedding, each of them still

on the line, *I need you more than want you and
I want you for all time,* yesterday, another storm,
a transformer blew on the line, the whole street
sparked blue, the lineman came to fix it around nine

and was up working into the morning, we peered out
the window, dared one another to go outside and serenade
him, *he's still on the line!* we wondered if climate change
has him busier than ever, wondered if he also wonders

how to pay his electric bill each month, despite so much
work, so much love, wondered if he also loves The Rhinestone
Cowboy the way we do, without irony, with a high tolerance
for schmaltz, wondered if he has someone he wants for all

time, and if I listen close enough, I begin to think of strangers
like him as people I know, I begin to think of people I know
as if they were strangers, but not in a sad way, it's a respectful
distance, full of love and mystery, the way I hope I know

anything, tethered to uncertainty, wanting for all time,
a great wedding song when I come to think of it,
I don't even remember hearing it at our wedding,
we were sparking blue every which way,

but our friends were still on the line, stoking the fire,
and when I think of it I can hear them now, still on the line,
a whiff of jasmine riding a September evening's breeze,
right around the time the temperature drops and the asphalt

is relieved of the sun, sends its warmth right back, the way
the guitar line blossoms out of the vocal, *still on the line,* the way
your love relieves me of my expectations on love, the way
a love song is also a work song, this labor of love, the only way.

Wichita Lineman

is it the sound   of my listen
ing of your song   ing is it self
sailing on time   serving to want
to wire or echo   to hear it again

Sestina for the Spinning Wheel

I believe in the ideal of chosen family,
but here I am, pumping all this blood.
Each its own heritage, each its own world.
Jimmy lives in both. I steer the wheel
toward West Virginia to research his life,
but I'm also looking for parts of mine.

I drive through mining country, excavating what was never mine
in my grandpa and Jimmy's hollers, where their families
worked in industry's hollowed-out hills to carve out a life.
Life, a tender hinge upon choice and blood –
swinging further open with each sharp turn, my wheels
eddying through the gorge. I listen to Iris DeMent's *Workin' On a World,*

and my ancestors' dreams rise up from the road. I think of Naomi Turner's world –
the men away fighting for the union when a confederate lit her house on fire, declared *mine.*
She emerged from the ash, defiant, holding up her smoking spinning wheel,
said, *anything but this.* This, her work, and this poem, mine, my quilt weaving family –
Naomi, Papaw, Jimmy, and my beloved riding shotgun – beyond blood –
quilting a garment from their stories with which to adorn my life,

though there are so many holes that need patching, so many questions to keep alive.
Ancestry.com told me about Naomi, even with so many Turners in this world,
though I know miners chances to tell stories didn't last long, so much blood,
my own great-grandfather killed at forty-four by slate fall inside the old mine
I pass by. The more I trace it, the more I find capital's shears trimming the family
tree – still I climb, stitch what threads I find through my loom, sweet spinning wheel,

spinning chosen family's anthems on my journey: Iris, Lucinda Williams' "Car Wheels
on a Gravel Road," Beverly Glenn-Copeland's "Ever New," Jimmy's "Life
Turned Her That Way," and his life turned me this way, toward Turners, family,
and closer to the circles of musical family in the outside world.
As a child I thought if I tried to overlap that I would lose mine,
but I work at the wheel, prick my finger, and the blood isn't changed by the bleeding.

I map a route to my great-grandfather's grave, backroads like veins of blood,
uncertain I'll find the way, dusty wheels
rolling off the dirt road to the little churchyard near the mine.
I read name after name in stone but can't find his to save my life,
people slow to rubberneck from the road, *what in the world
are these hippies doing here, surely they aren't family!*

And then my beloved wheels around – he's found the headstone, its own little world –
my dearest life choice paying respects to all this blood,
and we sew a new stitch in this family quilt: Papaw's, Naomi's, Jimmy's, my love's and mine.

Notes

Twin-lead cable is a two-pronged copper wire used to conduct radio frequencies. It is essential that the two copper strands are held a precise distance apart in order to conduct properly and not feed back.

Twin leads is also a style of dual lead guitar playing which, according to the Country Music Hall of Fame, was made popular by Dickens' band The Country Boys which included Jabbo Arrington and Grady Martin (and later, Jimmy "Spider" Wilson and Howard Rhoton).

"Twin Lead Cable" references the song "Up Above My Head I Hear Music in the Air" by Sister Rosetta Tharpe. This poem also contains a quote from an interview with Dickens conducted by Suzanne Higgins with West Virginia Public Broadcasting, which aired in 2007 and can be found on YouTube. The first lines of each couplet in the poem "Twin Lead Lines" are also fragmented quotes of Dickens in this interview.

The longrunning anagram poem at the top and bottom of each page, "Signal/Noise," includes phrases from the hymns "Come Thou Fount" and "Will the Circle Be Unbroken;" the poems "Island" and "Flying to Hanoi" by Muriel Rukeyser; Leonard Cohen's song "Bird on a Wire;" among my own lines of poetry and song lyrics. An anagram is a line made up entirely of rearranged letters from a previous line. The bottom lines are anagrams made up from the top lines.

"The O and the I" references the following Little Jimmy Dickens songs: "I'm Little But I'm Loud," "Take an Old Cold 'Tater (And Wait)," "Country Boy," "Are You Insured Beyond the Grave," "The Bible on the Table (and the Flag Upon the Wall)." The poem "Beyond" is an erasure of the lyrics from "Are You Insured Beyond the Grave," written by Joel Price and Oakie Jones. The poem "The Bible The Flag The Wall" is an erasure of the lyrics from "The Bible on the Table (and the Flag Upon the Wall)," written by George J. Bennett, Paul Cunningham, and Leonard Whitcup. The poem "If It Ain't One Thing It's Another" is titled after a song Dickens recorded, written by Boudleaux Bryant.

"One Side of an Interview with the Ghost of Little Jimmy Dickens" is after Hanif Abdurraqib's poem "One Side of an Interview with the Ghost of Marvin Gaye," which is after Eve L. Ewing. This poem references a plane crash that Little Jimmy Dickens survived in 1988. The totaled aircraft was a twin-engine plane.

"One Way" references Matthew 25:23 in the Bible as well as the song "Wild Thing," made popular by The Troggs.

"His High Note was My Low Note" borrows its title from a line in Diane Seuss' poem "Self-Portrait with Freddie M (Invention of Thunder)."

"My Life is Flying to Your Life" borrows its title from a line in Muriel Rukeyser's poem "Flying to Hanoi."

"What If" references the song "Coal Miner's Daughter" by Loretta Lynn.

"J&J's Market and Cafe" references painter and musician Peggy Snow. You can learn more about her work at pasrll.net/peggysnow/

"Listening to the Harvest" references "Heart of Gold" from Neil Young's album *Harvest*.

"Wichita Lineman" and "Still on the Line" are both inspired by Glen Campbell's recording of the Jimmy Webb song "Wichita Lineman."

The sonnet crown "O's Poetica" contains references to Matthew 19:24, Matthew 16:26, the hymn "How Great Thou Art," and borrows from a quote by theologian Matthew Fox: "Lose your soul and the world becomes solely a marketplace;" as well as a quote from Hildegard of Bingen: "We cannot live in aworld interpreted for us by others. An interpreted world is not a hope. Part of the terror is to take back our listening, to use our own voice, to see our own light. There is the music of Heaven in all things." The first sonnet in the crown also exists as lyrics to my song "I've Got the O's.

"Will the Magic Circle of Infinity Be Unbroken, Too?" references George Crumb's 1972 composition "Makrokosmos." I recommend looking it up to check out the score as well as recordings of the work.

"Song Cycle" alludes to a quote by Meister Eckhart: "God is the denial of denial."

The photo of Little Jimmy Dickens, Hank Williams, and Cowboy Copas on page 11 appears courtesy of the Country Music Hall of Fame. The author is unknown.

Acknowledgements

Gratitude to the editors at the journals where these poems first appeared:

Swing - "Before the glass breaks, a toast"
Quarter Notes - "Twin Lead Lines"
OEI: Aural Poetics - "Instructions for Writing a Country Song in Music City"
EcoTheo - "Listening to the Harvest"
Voicemail Poems - "Still on the Line"
museum of americana - "Beyond"
HAD - "We the Roost"
Noir Sauna - "Wichita Lineman" and "Making Do"
Fine Print Press - "The End"
Southern Cultures 31, no. 4: Country Music's Mythology, "After 96 Years of Business, Brown's Diner Begins Serving Impossible Burgers"

And to Freddy La Force at Vegetarian Alcoholic Press for publishing my chapbook, *Shape Note Singing,* which includes an earlier version of the poem "J&J's Market & Cafe."

I couldn't have imagined a more perfect home for this book than Third Man Books. My deepest gratitude to the whole Third Man team, including Amin Qutteineh, Abby Johnson, and Chet Weise. Thank you, Chet, for your gusto!

Thank you to Emily Hilliard, Sally Morgan, and Michelle Dove of SPINSTER Records for releasing my song "I've Got the O's" which contains several lines from "O's Poetica;" as well as my song "Will the Circle Be Unbroken" which includes a reading of "J&J's Market & Cafe." Special thanks to Emily for sharing so many insights into the folklore of West Virginia.

To Courtney Maum and Alice Hutchins with The Cabins: thank you for the dreamiest residency in Truth or Consequences, NM, which indelibly impacted this work. This writing period was also supported in part by a grant from Metro Nashville Arts Commission – thanks to them for believing in this work.

Overflowing gratitude to my brilliant Randolph family, especially Bea Troxel, LM Brimmer, Nicole Sessions, and Josh Nicolaisen; as well as my incisive, generous mentors: Layli Long Soldier, Diana Khoi Nguyen, Jos Charles, and Paige Lewis.

Everyday I'm thankful for my Nashville writing and music families; everyone at The Porch (especially Meg Wade and Susannah Felts) and the many beautiful musicians who appear in these poems either explicitly or in spirit (Peggy Snow, The Cherry Blossoms, In Place, the Springwater Writers Night-ers, and of course, my dear fellow Styrofoam Winos). Gratitude to all of the haunts mentioned here and all the people who make them special (big love to all who loved J&J's).

Mikey Swanberg – thank you for your generosity and keen eye. Katie Miller and Hilary Bell – this work would never have begun without you both – thank you for the warmth of your friendship and the unmatched care you bring to each word you encounter.

To my family: thank you for encouraging me to follow this calling; and to my ancestors and especially Little Jimmy Dickens: thank you for singing through the wires – I hope to honor your rich legacies of making do.

Trevor, my beloved: thank you for listening. It's my deepest joy to twin lead with you.

Photo by Abby Johnson

Lou Turner is a writer and musician (Styrofoam Winos, Ryan Davis & the Roadhouse Band) based in Nashville, TN. She holds an MFA in poetry from Randolph College and is the author of the chapbook *Shape Note Singing* (VA Press, 2021) as well as the editor of *Quarter Notes*, a literary magazine with a musical ear. Turner was a 2023 recipient of a solo artist residency from The Cabins, as well as a recipient of a Nashville Metro Arts Thrive Grant. The 2024 winner of The Porch Prize in Poetry, recent poems have appeared in OEI's Aural Poetics issue, *Voicemail Poems*, *The Continental Review*, *EcoTheo*, and elsewhere. Turner's latest solo record *Microcosmos* (SPINSTER) was named a Best Album of 2022 by NPR Music's Ann Powers. *Twin Lead Lines*—called "a veritable feat in symphonic composition" by Diana Khoi Nguyen—is her first book.

www.ingramcontent.com/pod-product-compliance
Lightning Source LLC
Chambersburg PA
CBHW051645120626

46551CB00015B/2225